The Economics and Politics of the Slowdown in Regulatory Reform

The Economics and Politics of the Slowdown in Regulatory Reform

Roger G. Noll

AEI-Brookings Joint Center for Regulatory Studies

WASHINGTON, D.C.

1999

Financial support from the Markle Foundation is gratefully acknowledged as are the comments by Robert W. Hahn, Robert E. Litan, and Clifford Winston on an earlier draft of this volume.

ISBN 0-8447-7139-2

1 3 5 7 9 10 8 6 4 2

The AEI Press
Publisher for the American Enterprise Institute
1150 17th Street, N.W.
Washington, D.C. 20036

ISBN 978-0-8447-7139-7

Contents

Foreword

This volume is one in a series commissioned by the AEI-Brookings Joint Center for Regulatory Studies to contribute to the continuing debate over regulatory reform. The series will address several fundamental issues in regulation, including the design of effective reforms, the impact of proposed reforms on the public, and the political and institutional forces that affect reform.

Many forms of regulation have grown dramatically in recent decades—especially in the areas of the environment, health, and safety. Moreover, expenditures in those areas are likely to continue to grow faster than the rate of government spending. Yet, the economic impact of regulation receives much less scrutiny than direct, budgeted government spending. We believe that policymakers need to rectify that imbalance.

The federal government has made substantial progress in reforming economic regulation—principally by deregulating prices and reducing entry barriers in specific industries. For example, over the past two decades consumers have realized major gains from the deregulation of transportation services. Still, policymakers can achieve significant additional gains from fully deregulating other industries, such as telecommunications and electricity.

While deregulating specific industries has led to substantial economywide gains, the steady rise in social regulation—which includes not only environmental, health, and safety standards but many other government-imposed rights and benefits—has had mixed results. Entrepreneurs increasingly face an assortment of employer mandates and legal liabilities that dictate decisions about products, payrolls, and personnel practices. Several scholars have questioned the wisdom of that expansion in social regulation. Some regulations, such as the phaseout of lead in gasoline, have been quite successful, while others, such as the requirement for safety caps on aspirin bottles, have led to increased risks. As those regulatory activities grow, so does the need to consider their implications more carefully.

We do not take the view that all regulation is bad or that all proposed reforms are good. We should judge regulations by their individual benefits and costs, which in the past have varied widely. Similarly, we should judge reform proposals on the basis of their likely benefits and costs. The important point is that, in an era when regulation appears to impose very substantial costs in the form of higher consumer prices and lower economic output, carefully weighing the likely benefits and costs of rules and reform proposals is essential for defining an appropriate scope for regulatory activity.

The debates over regulatory policy have often been highly partisan and ill-informed. We hope that this series will help illuminate many of the complex issues involved in designing and implementing regulation and regulatory reforms at all levels of government.

ROBERT W. HAHN
ROBERT E. LITAN
AEI-Brookings Joint Center
for Regulatory Studies

1

The Slowdown
of Regulatory Reform

From the mid-1970s until the mid-1980s, critics of the
U.S. regulatory system won a series of heady political
victories.[1] The most prominent examples were in economic regulation, where price and entry controls were virtually eliminated in transportation and hydrocarbon fuels
and made less restrictive in most other regulated industries.[2] In environmental, health, and safety regulation, important advances were made in increasing the flexibility of
regulation, such as by introducing limited forms of emissions trading[3] and by institutionalizing economic analysis
in major regulatory decisions through the regulatory review process in the Office of Management and Budget.[4]

Since the mid-1980s, however, victories have been fewer
and less complete. A few examples will illustrate the general point that regulatory reform is now progressing far
more slowly.

In environmental regulation, despite the success of
highly constrained emissions trading programs for air pol-
lutants and much more flexible trading systems for leaded
gasoline and chlorofluorocarbons, progress has been slow
in making existing emissions trading programs more flexible and extending emissions trading to other environmental problems.[5] In some cases stringent, inflexible new
regulatory requirements have been adopted, such as the
standards for auto emissions and airborne toxics in the
Clean Air Act Amendments of 1990[6] and the uncompro-

1

mising requirements of the Americans with Disabilities Act of 1990.[7] With respect to regulatory process, attempts to force agencies to take into account economic impact analyses of all new regulations have been unsuccessful.[8]

In economic regulation, one of the biggest targets—the Federal Maritime Commission—remains largely untouched. Most states have not gone beyond minimal federal requirements in allowing competition into electricity generation and still have little or no installed generation capacity that is accounted for by independent power producers.[9] When the Federal Communications Commission made the perfectly sensible decision to focus its regulation of long-distance telephone service solely on the one firm with market power, AT&T, the courts required the agency to engage in the costly and pointless regulation of AT&T's competitors. Congress, seeking to replace usage-based, long-distance access charges with a fixed monthly customer charge, also forced the FCC to backtrack.[10]

The Telecommunications Act of 1996, which I examine in some detail in this volume, illustrates the mixed and even dubious progress in recent regulatory policies. That legislation deregulates cable television, gives the Federal Communications Commission the power to overturn anticompetitive state regulations and to decide not to regulate if it deems a market sufficiently competitive, and formally adopts a policy of making local telephone service competitive. But the legislation also creates a multilayered, complex regulatory process not only for introducing competition, but also for using regulation to protect against the largely illusory myth that technological progress and competition somehow threaten "universal service"—the ubiquitous provision of telephone connections to virtually everyone. Notwithstanding its deregulatory and pro-competitive rhetoric, the main result of the act at the end of the millennium was several thousand pages of new FCC notices, reports, and orders and numerous lawsuits that delayed for several years the FCC's attempt to implement the act.

Those examples illustrate the pervasiveness and durability of extensive regulatory interventions. The purpose of this volume is to explore the political causes of the slowdown in regulatory reform. The strategy is, first, to set forth the key elements of the theory of policy change that have emerged from rational-actor models of political behavior; second, to identify some plausible causes of the loss of momentum in reform; and, third, to make some observations about how the momentum for reform might be regained.

With respect to the first question, I argue that four factors have contributed to the slowdown in reform. The most obvious is that many pending regulatory reform proposals deal with issues for which the direct relevance of economic analysis is controversial among elected officials. In addition, economists have intensified that problem by dramatically changing the role of economics in the policy process. Economic policy analysis has become more adversarial and discordant and thus has diverted attention from reform proposals that enjoy widespread professional agreement.

Two more general changes in the political sphere also have slowed the pace of regulatory reform: shrinking nonentitlement domestic expenditures and increasing emphasis on giving states more independence in policy implementation. The former has increased the relative importance of regulation as a means of delivering political favors to politically influential groups, and the latter has caused a conflict between improving the economic rationality of regulation and allowing regulation to be more responsive to state politics, where the pressure to use regulation as an instrument of redistribution is frequently greater than in the federal government.

With respect to the question about how momentum for reform could be regained, the most important force that is likely to cause further reform is simply the growing unwieldiness of regulation. Organized interests are more likely to fuel reform when they perceive greater gains from making the system more flexible and effective than from using the existing structure to pursue private gains. Economic analysis can facilitate that process by documenting the inefficiencies of poorly crafted regulations and cumbersome regulatory processes and instruments.

Economic analysis can be influential in promoting regulatory reform. But economists will be more successful in advancing reform if their policy advice is less adversarial, more consensual, more comprehensive, and more objective than the standard consulting report or partisan advocacy statement. Unfortunately, the latter has become the dominant method that economists use to communicate with regulatory policymakers.

2

Theories of Regulatory Reform

During the postwar era, the application of economic reasoning to politics and public policy formation has produced several important insights about factors that influence policy change. Here, I summarize those ideas and interpret them in the context of regulatory reform.[11]

The underlying premise of such an approach is that policy change occurs because most elected political officials find change in their interest because it either enhances their ability to maintain and extend their careers or comports with their personal policy preferences without damaging their political ambitions. In both cases the response of constituents to policy reform plays an important role. Elected leaders enhance their political careers (or, at least, do not undermine them) if a majority of their constituents perceive their actions to be more beneficial than harmful. Several decision-theoretic models have been developed to explore the implications of that hypothesis.[12]

Interest Groups and Capture

Initially, the economic theory of the politics of regulation emphasized forces that political scientists such as Bernstein and Lowi had identified earlier: regulation is primarily a means for delivering policy benefits to organized interests that experience a disproportionately large share of the consequences of a policy.[13] The core ideas in the economic version of that theory are based on the economics of political organization, originating with Anthony Downs and Mancur Olson[14] and extensively developed by Chicago School economists George Stigler, Sam Peltzman, and Gary Becker.[15]

The interest-group theory of regulation contains two key arguments. First, because undertaking activities to influence policy is expensive, only those with a high stake in a policy are likely to derive net benefits from attempting to influence it. Second, if people with the same stake in a policy form a political organization to achieve their common ends, as their numbers grow their political organization is increasingly likely to suffer from attempts by members to free ride—that is, not to pay their share of the costs of influencing policy. Consequently, smaller groups and groups already organized for another purpose are advantaged, if we hold the total stakes of all members constant.

In the simple theory of regulatory capture, a regulated industry has large per capita stakes, while customers and suppliers face small per capita stakes. Hence, the regulated industry is likely to become well organized to influence its own regulation so as to obtain regulations that advantage it relative to unorganized groups. More generally, if some but not all suppliers and customers experience concentrated effects, regulation can be expected to compromise their differences but collectively to advantage those groups relative to unorganized suppliers and customers.

According to the interest-group theory of regulation, reform takes place because organized interests turn against regulation.[16] Those who putatively benefit from regulation will advocate reform when their process costs of regulation are large compared with the benefits that those groups can extract from others. Those process costs have two components. One is the direct cost of participating in the regulatory process and complying with regulatory rules. The other, and usually larger, component is the indirect effect of regulation on the efficiency with which regulated firms respond to changes in technology, costs, and demand. By slowing the firms' appropriate response and by increasing its cost, regulation decreases the efficiency of firms.

An attack on regulation by the groups that are most influential in making regulatory policy may occur if unanticipated events either increase the costs or reduce the benefits of regulation to its former advocates. Three types of such changes can have one or both of those effects.

First, so many groups that regulation affects may become organized that the costs of negotiating and implementing compromises among them become excessively cumbersome and expensive and so not worth the rents that those groups can extract from others. Regulating a large number of heterogeneous firms is costly, not just because it requires collecting and analyzing a great deal of data, but also because it requires a great deal of work assessing the effects of proposed regulatory changes on participants in the industry. Good examples of areas in which large numbers of firms operating under different circumstances and with different costs caused price regulation to be cumbersome and expensive are natural gas, oil, and trucking.

If the number of regulated firms grows, we can expect the process costs of regulation to increase more than in proportion to the number of firms, and those costs will thus reduce the net benefits of regulation to its proponents. An increase in the number of regulated firms can arise through the growth in demand for a regulated service that increases the prospective profitability of entry into the regulated market by excluded firms. As the demand for a regulated product grows, the prospective profits of entry will eventually swamp the process costs of gaining permission to enter. And, as more firms enter, regulation becomes more cumbersome and expensive. Examples of that process are the entry of cable television firms and nonscheduled and charter airlines in the 1970s.

Second, technological change or entrepreneurial creativity may lead to competition that undermines the ability of regulated interests to extract rents from unorganized groups. The source of that competition may be unregulatable competitive actions by regulated firms or entry into unregulated activities that can substitute for regulated ones. An example of the first type of competition was the largely unregulatable service competition among airlines that shared price-regulated routes.[17] Service competition eroded the excess profits of those routes and thereby eliminated the reason of some airlines for favoring regulation.

Because the regulatory process is costly and inflexible, when regulated firms face competition from unregulated firms, the former are competitively handicapped and so are likely to experience a diminished opportunity for extracting rents. An example arose from the convergence of telephone and computer technologies, which allowed many major business customers of telephone service to acquire internal communications systems that reduced their usage of regulated local phone service. After the Federal Communications Commission decided not to regulate private networks and computer services, regulated telephone monopolies began to experience limited competition to which they could not effectively respond while remaining regulated. As a result, local telephone companies have lost a large share of the access connections between intensive telecommunications users and long-distance carriers.

Third, if a large fraction of the groups affected by a regulatory policy become organized, the opportunity for extracting rent from the remaining groups may not offset the costs of participating in the regulatory process. For example, if income growth and technological change increase the per capita stakes of the customers of firms subject to economic regulation, the demand side is increasingly likely to become organized, thereby reducing the asymmetry of representation in the policy process. Of course, if the nature of technology in the regulated industry allows it to be reasonably competitive, eventually both sides can mutually agree that they are better off with less regulation. The evolution of surface freight transportation illustrates that pattern with respect to large shippers and railroads, although most trucking firms and the Teamsters Union fought deregulation to the end.

Interest-group theory is not exactly clear about the outcome when some organized groups want to retain regulation but others oppose it. The political science version of interest-group theory emphasizes the importance of a united front among advocates of a policy. If both sides are roughly equally well organized, and one side is united while the other is divided, political actors can expect a net political gain only by siding with the united front. In the economic regulatory domain, the political science argument leads to the prediction that if the regulated industry is divided about whether regulation should be relaxed and if user groups are well organized and oppose regulation, regulatory reform should be victorious. In the environmental regulatory domain, if environmentalists are divided about the wisdom of a regulatory approach that is more efficient and if regulated firms advocate that reform, then it should take place.

The economic version of interest-group theory is more complicated in that it takes into account the magnitude of the stakes for each side. Initially, Stigler imagined that something akin to an auction for policy took place, whereby the organized group that had the largest net benefit from change would win the policy struggle. In general, as argued by Becker, such a process should favor a policy outcome that is reasonably efficient, because, if regulation is not efficient, the gains for the beneficiaries are smaller than the losses of those who suffer from inefficiency. Hence, if all sides are reasonably equally organized politically, regulation ought to be relatively efficient.

Following Becker's argument, if two groups on the same side of a regulatory issue disagree about regulatory policy and if both are well organized, the group proposing the more efficient alternative should be favored, since its proposal generates more surplus for distribution among organized interests and to policymakers.

Peltzman has applied the interest-group approach in attempting to explain the economic deregulation of the late 1970s and early 1980s.[18] The model seems to work relatively well in explaining federal regulatory reforms in some cases, but less well in other areas. For example, Peltzman concludes that the interest-group theory does not adequately explain deregulation in long-distance telephone service and trucking.

Even in the more problematic cases, interest-group analysis sheds some light. The two examples of local telephone service and emissions trading demonstrate both the usefulness and limitations of that model.

Telecommunications. In the case of local access, potential competitors and many business user groups have long advocated the end of franchised monopoly in local telephone service. In essence, those groups propose that long-distance carriers, cable television companies, and specialized providers of internal networks and access to long-distance carriers be allowed to interconnect with local telephone companies and to sell local access service competitively. Willing providers and organized users who favor competition were certainly stronger and more numerous for local telephone service in the 1980s than for long-distance service in the 1960s.

Despite the seemingly favorable politics, the pace of regulatory reform has been much slower in the case of local telephony. Local telephone companies have been almost completely successful in preventing competition in ordinary local telephone service. Although some states began to allow alternative local access arrangements in the mid-1990s, no state fully relaxed entry barriers and worked out competitively neutral policies for interconnecting competing local telephone companies until the late 1990s.

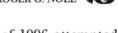

The Telecommunications Act of 1996 attempted to speed the development of local competition by extending federal jurisdiction over interconnection regulation and mandating the FCC to issue guidelines for state regulators that specify how to construct competitively neutral rules for interconnection.[19] Nevertheless, the act preserved for state regulators the task of developing procompetitive regulations and created a more elaborate regulatory system to protect universal service.

On the plus side, the act phased out by 1999 the expensive, largely unsuccessful attempt to reregulate charges for cable television service (section 301(b)) and reversed the court ruling that prevented the FCC from deregulating carriers that lacked market power (section 401). The act also contains provisions that facilitate competitive entry in local access by requiring local exchange carriers to provide nondiscriminatory interconnection, unbundled access elements, and collocation to competitors (section 251(a)) and by mandating that states eliminate barriers to entry against both facilities-based and resale local access providers (section 253(a)).

Other provisions in the act are exceedingly regulatory in both process and objectives. In setting forth procompetitive policies for interconnection, the act also created a new, exceedingly complex multilayered regulatory structure. The act asserted federal jurisdiction over the rules for interconnecting competitive telephone companies (sections 252(e)(6) and 253(d)) and provided a long list of conditions that interconnection agreements must satisfy (sections 251(b) and 251(c)). But the act also created a new regulatory monster by preserving some discretion for state regulators in developing interconnection rules, subject to FCC guidelines and court supervision. In addition, the standards for interconnection requirements are vague, including even the classic "public interest, convenience, and necessity" clause as guidance to state regulators about interconnection rules (section 252(e)(2)(A)(ii)).

Thus, the act set up a process that invites years, if not decades, of complex legal wrangling over the details of local access competition, which in turn raised the cost and slowed the pace of competitive entry. For example, it took almost three years to the day for the Supreme Court to rule that the FCC had the authority under the act to adopt policies that states must follow in regulating prices for interconnection and resale of the components of local telephone service—the so-called unbundled network elements. And, as the new millennium dawns, the courts still have not clarified the FCC's authority in setting forth conditions under which the Bell operating companies may offer long-distance service and in establishing a method for financing the act's universal service requirements.

An important flaw in the act is that it retains much of the incoherency of the jurisdictional separation of state and federal authority. Technically, any division between state and federal authority is arbitrary because the telecommunications system ought to be, and recently actually has become, a seamless network. So-called local access is also access to long-distance connections, and long-distance networks are not engineered so that intrastate and interstate calls are distinct services. Indeed, carriers make the current distinctions among local, intrastate long-distance, and interstate calls only because regulation forces them to do so, at considerable cost. The act recognizes that fact in two ways. First, the act states the objective that all parts of the industry should be competitive and that the market, not regulators, should determine whether the optimal organizational structure of a telecommunications firm is to offer all services, including television. Second, rightly or wrongly, the act states the objective that all areas—rural and urban, rich and poor—should have the same range of services. But the act then continues to give state regulators a major role in fashioning a policy that is intended to produce a homogeneous national service.

That jurisdictional division is problematic for two basic reasons. First, state politics inevitably makes state regulation parochial, favoring interests that are politically important within the state over interests that are physically located elsewhere. Especially in small states, there simply is no political payoff in assisting national telecommunications firms in competing more effectively against local telephone companies and facilitating e-commerce from the likes of Amazon.com at the expense of local retailers. Second, because states differ in their underlying economic and demographic structure, different groups will be influential in regulatory policy across different states. Hence, the vision of a seamless, homogeneous national system is inconsistent with having each state influence the design of the foundation of that network, which is the connection of customers to the system. Not surprisingly, many of the legal challenges to the act and to the FCC's attempt to implement it arise from state regulators who have either challenged the law of the FCC directly or promulgated regulations that are inconsistent with the act or FCC rules, thus forcing regulated firms to sue to resolve the conflict.

The new telecommunications act created another regulatory problem in its universal service provisions. The act set up a highly regulatory process for defining and making available universal service. First, the act created an open-ended definition of universal service—it could easily include cable television and mobile telephones within a few years—and an open-ended commitment to subsidize those services in high-cost, sparsely settled regions. The universal service subsidy is not tied to either the financial needs of customers or the demand for those services in subsidized areas. Thus, the act could transfer enormous financial burdens from nationwide telephone customers to wealthy residents of sparsely settled areas and could pay a large fraction of the costs for capabilities that customers in those areas do not want. Second, by requiring federal rate averaging and by permitting rate averaging in the states for the purpose of financing universal service subsidies, the act invites rigid price regulation that would prevent price competition in core services. Those provisions invite state and federal regulators to reregulate some deregulated services and to cut back on their use of incentive regulation systems, such as price caps, to implement an effective scheme of cross-subsidization for universal service.

The act reveals a more general legislative schizophrenia. For two decades economic regulatory policy has been based on the proposition that most, maybe even all, infrastructural industries could be structurally competitive. At the same time, policymakers have been unable to give up regulatory control in many of those industries. When the time comes for writing the legislation, too frequently legislators put aside the objective of promoting competition in a political attempt to allocate advantages among organized interests that requires establishing a continuing regulatory process to protect any interest from suffering an excessive financial loss from competition. Of course, that approach to reform runs a substantial risk of replacing a monopoly with a cartel, thereby forfeiting the benefits to most consumers of structural competition.

Emissions Trading. The old regulatory bargain between established industries and environmentalists included draconian "new source performance standards" that imposed expensive permit and compliance costs on new industrial facilities. Usually, the compliance cost to attain any given level of emissions control is much lower for a new facility than for an established one. Consequently, those harsh standards protected established facilities against entry by more efficient competitors. That arrangement initially benefited environmentalists as well, for imposing standards that would have bankrupted many companies and left their workers unemployed was not politically feasible. Hence, environmentalists could reasonably have believed that they would attain greater emissions reductions in the short run by protecting old facilities against entry.

As time passed, changes in demand, technology, and international trade undermined the value of that arrangement for both sides. Established facilities grew increasingly obsolete and less able to compete effectively against imports. Firms owning those facilities sought to expand or to introduce new technology and faced the same entry barriers from the new, rigorous standards because they applied to any significant renovation of an established facility. Environmentalists experienced reduced opportunities for imposing additional emissions controls because of the diminished rents the new standards created. Consequently, both industry and some environmental organizations saw increasing value in more flexible approaches to emissions controls that led to the introduction of emissions trading. The pace of reform has been very slow, however.

The political response to the success of the early experiments with trading is disappointing. The procedures for trading air pollution permits remain highly constrained and inefficient. In nearly all cases trading cannot be used to avoid compliance with the new source performance standards, although the gap between standards for new and established facilities has virtually disappeared in areas that are severely polluted. Progress in advancing the use of trading has been glacially slow despite support from many industrial and environmental groups as well as economists.

As in telecommunications reform, environmental regulation grants "front-line" jurisdiction for implementing most regulatory policy changes to state and local authorities. The most important victory for reformers was the provision in the Clean Air Act Amendments of 1990 that opened the door for the use of emissions markets to control air pollution and created a national market for sulfur dioxide emissions from coal-fired electric generation facilities for the purposes of reducing acid rain. But the amendments left to state and local regulators the task of deciding whether and, if so, how to introduce emissions trading to control localized air pollution. Unfortunately, in no case have state and local regulators adopted the kind of sweeping emissions trading system that economists, even those who are ardent environmentalists, recommend. The problem lies in the unbalanced politics that those regulators face.

The implementation of emissions trading in Los Angeles provides an especially poignant example.[20] As almost goes without saying, *Los Angeles* has become a synonym for *smog* as the city has long suffered from the worst air quality in the United States—although a few other cities are now threatening to challenge Los Angeles's long-dominant position. Perhaps less well known is the fact that, in the prereform era, Los Angeles also had the most stringent emissions regulations in the country and a regulatory authority, the South Coast Air Quality Management District, that generally received good marks for the efficiency of its regulations. Nevertheless, by the mid-1980s, it had become painfully obvious that traditional regulation could never achieve the goal of healthful air without causing enormous economic disruption. Not surprisingly, when the 1990 Clean Air Act Amendments were passed, the SCAQMD immediately instituted the process of replacing its elaborate system of source-specific technical regulations with an emissions trading system.

Initially, the goal was to apply emissions trading to all significant components of smog and to all sources. Historically, the SCAQMD had enjoyed minimal success in regulating small businesses, industries that were subject to intense competition from firms in other regions, and consumer products, such as oven cleaners, cosmetics, and outdoor barbecue grills. By 1990, when automobiles and most large, stationary sources were intensively regulated, those sources collectively accounted for nearly half the air pollution in Los Angeles and offered many relatively low-cost opportunities for reducing emissions. Thus, initially the SCAQMD, with support from both the intensively regulated firms and several environmental groups, embarked on a plan to use emissions trading to bring the uncontrolled and weakly regulated sources into the system of air pollution control.

After several years, those plans were abandoned. Emissions trading was implemented only for controlling sulfur oxides and nitrogen oxides from large sources that were already heavily regulated. Control of volatile organic compounds remained the province of technical standards that were applied only to large industrial processes and a few consumer products. The basic reason is that the Clean Air Act Amendments of 1990 had no effect on the local politics of regulation. Sources that had the political clout to escape costly standards also had the political clout to resist being regulated through the back door by being folded into an emissions trading program that had the goal of significantly reducing air pollution. Opponents of those plans painted the bleak picture of consumers' paying $10 for deodorant and for dry-cleaning a shirt and of the loss of hundreds of thousands of jobs among small businesses. Local political leaders, who control the SCAQMD, responded by putting into abeyance the implementation of emissions trading on a broad scale. As a result, emissions trading in Los Angeles will not be permitted to eliminate the vast disparity in abatement costs between heavily regulated and largely unregulated sources of the same pollutants.

The Los Angeles reform fell far short of initial hopes and expectations because reform was bundled with rearranging the benefits and costs of the regulatory system. In environmental, health, and safety regulation, the object of reform has been to make policy more efficient but not to deregulate. If reform seeks both to make compliance less expensive, given the regulatory objective, and to increase the stringency of the overall policy, then reform is very likely either to fail or to be much less complete. Two factors lead to that result. The first is that an inefficient system of regulatory standards is not some sort of unlucky fluke, but the outcome of conscious decisions in a political environment that accords greater weight to some interests than to others. The second is that if one object of reform is to make products, workplaces, and the environment more healthful and safe, the inevitable consequence is to threaten to impose new costs on those who have thus far escaped them, regardless of how efficient the reformed system promises to be. Thus, those who successfully oppose applying traditional regulation will also oppose the reform, and we have no reason to believe that they will be any less successful in the new regime than in the old. As a result, the second goal of reform, significant improvements in health and safety, limits the attainability of the first goal, to minimize the costs of regulatory compliance with any given standard for health and safety.

Local implementation of reform makes reform less likely because local officials are subject to one form of political pressure: the possibility that local citizens will be disadvantaged relative to others in neighboring localities in terms of either a higher cost of living (for example, cosmetics' having higher prices in Los Angeles than in San Diego) or the loss of jobs (for example, glass bottle manufacturing's moving from Los Angeles to the Central Valley or even out-of-state to Phoenix). As one ascends the hierarchy of government, those localized distributive concerns surely do not disappear, but they do become less significant politically. Hence, reform is likely to be more difficult to implement if local authorities play a significant role in implementing it.

3

Causes of Slow Progress

Superficially, an important element of the slow pace in reforming telecommunications and environmental regulation is that regulators, in implementing reform, reveal a preference not to introduce policies that vastly diminish their roles. For example, in the development and implementation of emissions trading in Los Angeles (Project RECLAIM), the South Coast Air Quality Management District, itself an advocate of reform, met significant resistance from both the California Air Resources Board and the Region Nine office of the Environmental Protection Agency. In general, as Crandall and Winston have argued, state and federal regulators can be regarded as constituting a relevant interest group that seeks to protect its interests—in this case, jobs and authority to control the behavior of regulated firms.[21] That explanation is incomplete, however, because regulators are appointed and derive their power from statutes, both of which emanate from elected politicians. Whereas regulators enjoy policy discretion, they cannot stray excessively far from the policies preferred by a majority of elected officials without risking punishment and reversal.[22]

During the initial wave of reforms from the mid-1970s until 1980, Congress passed statutes that reduced the formal authority of regulatory agencies, and presidents appointed regulators who were committed to reducing the influence of their agencies. For example, the Civil Aeronautics Board deregulated a great deal of the airline industry before Congress ratified and extended those policies by passing legislation that phased out regulation and eventually abolished the agency.[23]

The case of the CAB illustrates the superficiality of the argument that regulators constitute an effective self-preserving interest. If one observes an agency persistently hamstringing reform, the explanation lies not in the interest of the agency, but in the willingness of elected political officials to allow an agency to behave in that way. In the end, elected officials must not feel threatened by persisting in those policies, despite agreement among the relevant interest groups that change is warranted. In the case of Project RECLAIM, the resistance of state and federal regulators was rather quickly (if painfully) overcome when political leaders and EPA headquarters supported reform. Cases in which regulators persist in blocking reform require a deeper political explanation and motivate exploring other developments in the rational-actor theory of policy formation.

Rational Ignorance and the Role of Information

Although rarely applied to regulation—or, indeed, to any specific area of policy—the implications of imperfect information about the consequences of political actions were first explored before the development of the economics of political organization. Downs was the first to propose a theory of the interactions between voters and candidates for office that was based on imperfectly informed voter decisions about the policies that candidates would adopt.[24] That theory hypothesizes that voters will not base voting decisions on the positions of candidates on any particular issue unless they perceive a large difference in expected personal net benefits between the positions advocated by the candidates. The two sufficient conditions for voters to perceive a difference between candidates are that the issue is important to them and that the difference between the two candidates on the issue is substantial. Whether the second condition is satisfied depends on the information available to voters: do the candidates propose different policy actions, and is their difference in proposed actions likely to have a significant effect on policy outcomes?

The acquisition of an informed opinion requires undertaking a sequence of costly actions, beginning with the study of cause-effect relations and ending with the personal processing of information within the context of an individual voter's preferences and interests. The most important insight of the information-theoretic approach to politics is the observation that voters are extremely unlikely to bear all the costs of being informed on all issues. If citizens see political participation as a means to maximize their expected policy payoff, they will decide whether to become informed by comparing the costs of information with the likely policy effect of their being better informed. Because a single vote has virtually zero probability of affecting the outcome of an election and thereby shaping policy, it also has virtually zero expected benefit to the voter. Hence, significant personal investment in information is highly unlikely to be rewarded by an increase in the personal net benefits of policy.

The preceding argument does not imply that voters will always be ignorant. Instead, it focuses attention on other mechanisms by which voters become informed or at least vote as if they were informed.[25]

First, voters may consume politically relevant products from professional information providers and thereby derive the ability to cast an informed vote as a byproduct of their consumption activities. For example, voters consume information by reading newspapers, watching television news programs, or reading books, rather than by explicitly investing in those activities to improve their ability to vote according to their policy preferences. Or they may inform themselves because they believe that having a better understanding of government will enable them to foresee policy changes more accurately and to respond more effectively when change occurs. On the other hand, if the motive for information acquisition is primarily consumption, voters may have a tendency to consume material that reinforces their prior beliefs and prejudices, in which case the acquisition of more information does not necessarily lead to political participation that is more informed.

Second, an activity that is closely related to consuming information products is receiving propagandistic information from interested participants in the political process. If voters acquire information inadvertently and do not believe that their own political actions are consequential, the information they acquire and the decisions that are based on it will not reflect optimizing behavior on their part. In particular, if information is biased and is incompletely processed (only enjoyable processing is undertaken), those who are willing to pay to provide selective (and entertaining) messages can systematically and persistently mislead a voter. Of course, that phenomenon applies to both the standard information industry and to the industry providing biased information. The former, however, would tend to reinforce erroneous assumptions about how the world works, whereas the latter is more likely to change people's beliefs in perverse ways.

Third, a politically active group to which a voter belongs may make the individual's cost of information insignificant by spreading that cost across all members of the group and telling each member how to vote, on the basis of the consensus preferences among members on issues pertaining to their common interests. Such a process fits in well with the interest-group theory of policy choice because it provides another role for organizations to play in mobilizing homogeneous groups.

A nice feature of the information-theoretic approach to politics is that it preserves a place for the intrepid policy analyst. Truly independent, objective policy analysis can influence voters along all three pathways. The work of the policy analyst may be popularized, or political officials and interest groups may hire policy analysts to develop analyses that use information to support their positions. In either case, the importance of the information derived from policy analysis is that it causes voters to update their assessments of the policy positions of candidates and their decisions about whom to support.

Informational imperfections also play a role in the policy choices of elected officials. The idea here is that elected officials, like voters, are imperfectly informed about how their actions will influence their constituents and, hence, their electoral fortunes. Like voters, elected officials could decide to attempt to be informed about everything; limits of time and resources preclude doing so, however. Alternatively, elected officials can delegate the duty to be informed. In some cases, they rely on information from organized constituency groups, which have an incentive to become informed on behalf of their group members and to reflect their members' preferences.[26] In other cases, they can delegate the task of collecting and evaluating information to a bureaucracy.

Recent developments in the theory of delegation to agencies have emphasized how administrative procedures influence policy outcomes by organizing the flow of information to bureaucratic decisionmakers.[27] According to that view, one purpose of administrative procedures is to assign weights to different types and sources of information, and even to alternative systems of values that might be used to inform policy decisions.[28] For example, rules of standing and rights of judicial review determine whose information must be given serious consideration in reaching a decision, and burdens and standards of proof determine the difficulty a proponent of change will face in reforming a regulatory policy.

The information-theoretic approach sheds some light on both the initial regulatory reform movement and the subsequent slowdown. In most cases, the first wave of reform proposals was to deregulate industries that were al-

ready structurally competitive in that several firms oper-
ated in at least some markets. Economic research played a
role, because, in the 1960s and 1970s, numerous studies
demonstrated the economic inefficiencies arising from such
regulation.[29] The proposals emanating from those economic
policy analyses were primarily to reduce the scope of regulation, not to change its character.

By contrast, many of the reform proposals on the
agenda in the 1990s are not based on a desire to deregulate, but instead to reform the regulatory process. For example, mandatory benefit-cost analysis in environmental,
health, and safety regulation is a procedural reform within
a continuing regulatory system. The examples discussed
above in which reform began in the earlier period but
slowed abruptly in the latter period—emissions trading and
local utility services—are also ones in which immediate
reforms deal primarily with the process. Emissions trading
would not cause environmental regulation to disappear,
just the aspect of it that sets source-specific technical standards. Reforming the regulation of electric utilities and
local telephone companies might eventually induce enough
entry for deregulation to be plausible, but the immediate
proposals are for procedural reforms. Price caps, permission for vertical integration, competitively neutral interconnection, and facilities sharing among competitors are
examples.

From the perspective of elected political officials, regulatory methods and procedures are not simply a means for
improving the efficiency of regulation. Elected political
officials naturally want to control policy. Because they cannot make all policy decisions and must delegate some authority to civil servants, their main concern in constructing
agencies is to avoid policy outcomes, conceptualized as who
wins and who loses, that are not consistent with their own
policy preferences. The primary purposes of regulatory
structure and process are to allocate influence among
groups represented in the regulatory process and to pro-

tect elected political officials from bureaucrats' policy decisions that are inconsistent with the purposes of regulatory legislation. Whereas a procedural reform plausibly could increase efficiency, it could also mean loss of political control of who wins a regulatory dispute. Likewise, if the existing structure biases regulatory policy in favor of a particular interest group, that group may still prefer deregulation to regulation but be wary of fiddling with the process.

To illustrate that point, consider the case of mandatory benefit-cost analysis in environmental, health, and safety regulation. The basis for a belief that mandatory benefit-cost analysis will improve the performance of regulatory agencies is the information-theoretic approach to understanding bureaucratic delegation. In its present incarnation, regulatory review in the Office of Management and Budget has no clear, formal means of influencing decisions other than by increasing the amount of relevant information in the decisionmaking process. That rather minimal formal role can influence outcomes if either the agency leaders are interested in improving the efficiency of their policies or a well-represented interest makes use of the information to oppose, and eventually perhaps to appeal, an inefficient proposal by the agency.

Economic analysis would have a greater role if agencies were required to base their decisions on an economic analysis that used standardized economic assumptions, methods, and information (for example, the discount rate or the value of life) and to bear the burden of proof if a decision overrides the results of such an analysis. If a benefit-cost analysis were objective, in the sense of being based on the best available relevant information, that change in the formal status of economic analysis would further advantage groups favoring policies that are more efficient than the policies actually adopted.

Unfortunately, the most well-organized interests are not necessarily the ones that would benefit from efficient policies. Moreover, if citizens are poorly informed about the true nature of a regulatory problem, they may create a popular demand for an inefficient policy, in which case voters and elected officials see the failure to adopt it as ideological unresponsiveness, not the result of detached analysis.

Of course, economic policy analysis is frequently biased, in which case enhancing its formal role does not necessarily enhance efficiency. Consider the case in which agencies must base decisions on information supplied by participants in the regulatory process and either information or representation is uneven among interests. In that case, increasing the weight accorded to benefit-cost analysis will increase the importance of representation bias and will add to the weight accorded to the group that possesses crucial private information.

Policy analysts tend to appreciate insufficiently the problem of bias in analysis. If neither citizens nor elected officials have the skills, let alone the time, to evaluate the quality of economic policy analysis, a decision to give analysts greater policy influence raises some quite rational fears that the policies favored by policy analysts will reflect the values and preferences of the analysts rather than a comprehensive, objective assessment of the issue.

We can hardly expect the growth and content of economic consulting to have ameliorated that concern. Active participation by consulting economists as advocates in the policy process has elevated the content and rigor of policy debates, regulatory decisionmaking, and litigation, which is all to the good. But consulting activity also is likely to have reduced the willingness of noneconomists to delegate formal responsibility to economists. The latter effect arises from the fact that if both parties to a dispute hire competent economists, their consulting reports are likely to be in almost complete conflict and to make no serious attempt to reconcile opposing arguments.

The present reality of discourse among economists lies

in stark contrast to the virtual unanimity among professional economists concerning the desirability of deregulation in transportation, hydrocarbon fuels, and the financial sector. From the perspective of an elected official, newspaper reporter, or interested citizen, all of whom are unlikely to be able to evaluate consulting reports—much less to integrate them into a coherent view of a proposed change in policy—the cumulative effect of discord is to foster the belief that delegation to economists may cause unreliable and unpredictable policy decisions that depend primarily on who is assigned to the job of analyzing a particular regulatory proposal.

Political unresponsiveness and politically unpopular ideological bias are potential hazards of proposals to change the way regulation is done, as opposed to eliminating regulation altogether. To succeed, reform proposals must come to grips with the multiple political purposes of regulatory structure and process, and the rational fear of antidemocratic delegation of policy influence to experts.

4

Mass Politics

The economic analysis of political phenomena has always been proposed as a partial theory. It is a story about sources of bias away from an outcome that would result from a hypothetical unbiased aggregation of citizen preferences. One should bear in mind that citizens engage in political participation for a host of reasons unrelated to their association with organized interests and have strongly held views about policy that are not related to their sources of income and their major personal consumption expenditures. Hence, another factor that may have affected the pace of regulatory reform is changes in other political issues that have a spillover effect on regulation.

Conventional wisdom holds that the most important political trend in the United States since 1980 is that the electorate has become generally more conservative. Because a tenet of conservatism is to reduce substantially the extent of regulation, the slowdown in reform since the early 1980s is perhaps surprising.

The difficulty with drawing conclusions about specific policies from general political trends is that to do so assumes that the shift in public political attitudes is more or less uniform across all issues. Poll data indicate that such is not the case. The extent to which citizens express agreement with conservative policies varies enormously across policy issues. One policy that still commands a large majority of support is environmental regulation. Whereas that support does not imply that environmental regulation cannot be significantly reformed, it does mean that elected

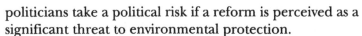

politicians take a political risk if a reform is perceived as a significant threat to environmental protection.

To my knowledge, no long-term polling data exist for most other specific areas of regulation, and in any event, regardless of public opinion, most specific areas of regulation are not particularly salient to most voters. Indeed, the general lack of significant public interest in specific areas of regulation is the basis for the economic theory of regulation, which emphasizes capture by organized interests at the expense of citizens in general. Consequently, to incorporate general political trends into the analysis, one must look for more specific issues that have some direct bearing on regulation but that are more general than any specific area of regulation.

One such issue is the increased emphasis in recent years on greater devolution of policy responsibilities to state and local government. The federal structure of the American government is very unusual, and the consensus view among political scientists is that a system in which different levels of government exercise significant, independent power is probably not stable.[30] The logic of the conclusion is that if the national government possesses the legal authority to control a policy, the factions that control the national government will insist on using that authority to force lower governments to adhere to the policy that is favored at the national level. Even if the national government does not possess the legal authority, it can use its superior military power over one of its subunits to achieve its will by force.

In the history of the United States, the role of states has ebbed and flowed in all policy areas, including regulation. Although the New Deal period is regarded as one in which considerable power was centralized in the national government, most New Deal statutes were generally deferential to the states. For example, states were given important roles in implementing nearly all New Deal social programs except for Social Security. In addition, New Deal regulatory statutes gave the states greater authority over intrastate activities of regulated utility industries than were contained in the earlier statutes for regulating railroads and pipelines.

In 1886, the Supreme Court held on constitutional grounds that states are precluded from regulating any business that jointly offers both interstate and intrastate service unless explicitly given the authority to do so by a federal statute. Subsequent regulatory statutes, such as the Interstate Commerce Act, delegated some regulatory responsibility to the states but gave federal regulators the authority to override state decisions. In contrast, the New Deal regulatory statutes regulating telecommunications, natural gas, airlines, and trucks created a confusing system of joint jurisdiction over intrastate activities and gave state regulators independent authority to regulate intrastate activities, even if those activities could not be separated, technically and economically, from interstate services. The Supreme Court has given varying and mutually inconsistent statutory interpretations of those laws in considering attempts by regulators at one level in the federal hierarchy to act contrary to decisions by regulators at another level.

In recent years, the view that more authority should be given to state and local governments has found expression in numerous areas of policy. Most of the action has been taken by either regulators or the courts, as appointees to agencies and, especially, to the bench have expanded the scope of state regulation. Two actions have been taken through statutes. The Cable Television Consumer Protection and Competition Act of 1992, which reregulated cable television, reinstated some regulatory authority over cable by state and local government. The Telecommunications Act of 1996 gave the FCC more authority over states in regulating interconnection arrangements among local access providers, although the act is sufficiently complicated and ambiguously worded that the ultimate effect of those provisions is uncertain. And, while the act deregulated cable television, it retained considerable de facto regulatory authority for local governments in negotiating franchise agreements—authority that has long since disappeared in franchising telecommunications and other utility services.

The dilemma posed by the trend toward more state and local authority is that devolution can work against regulatory reform, as illustrated by the discussions of telecommunications and emissions trading. State and local governments are subject to the same kinds of representation biases as the federal government, but in the former case one additional bias is present: the absence of an incentive to be politically responsive to organized groups in other areas that sell within the state or local jurisdiction. Whereas state and local governments are generally prohibited from erecting barriers to interstate trade, they are relatively free to use regulation to discriminate against people from other jurisdictions. An excellent example is a practice only recently attacked in telecommunications, which was to set higher long-distance access charges for terminating calls than for initiating them. That price structure is a means of taxing people outside the state, since all originating calls are placed from within a state but a large proportion of terminating calls are placed by people from outside the state. Precisely the same tendency has been observed in pricing international telephone calls.[31]

Regulatory reform generally has gained more political momentum in the federal government, most likely because a source of political benefits from regulation is available to state and local authorities—discrimination against residents and businesses from other jurisdictions—that is not available to federal officials. Thus, if a state or local government essentially reflects the mixture of economic interests of the federal government, it will be, on balance, less likely to undertake reform. Of course, that conclusion does not mean that all states and localities oppose reform, or even that all are less reform-minded than the federal government. If a state, city, or county contains an unusually large concentration of well-organized user groups that advocate reform, those groups may be more successful in their home state than in Washington. But, on balance, lower levels of government are likely to be more parochial, thus leading to greater use of regulation to benefit local constituencies.

5

The Future of Reform

The economic and political causes of the regulatory reform movement are far from completely understood, so strong conclusions about the likely future path to reinvigorated reform are hardly warranted. Nevertheless, some conclusions seem plausible enough to be worthy of consideration.

First, although something approaching consensus among interested parties in favor of reform is neither necessary (trucking) nor sufficient (emissions trading) to induce reform, such a consensus does appear to increase the probability that reform will be successful.

Second, when a regulated sector is divided, the most likely outcome is a compromised, gradual reform that appears more to divide the baby than to introduce economic efficiency. Political actors do not like to take the risk that a significant fraction of an industry will be significantly harmed by a reform.[32] For that reason, reform is likely to be protracted so that it can be halted or reversed before great damage has been done. Examples are the slow pace at which competition has been introduced in telecommunications for the past three decades and the gradual process of relaxing regulatory restrictions on cable television during the 1970s and early 1980s.

Third, during the past thirty years, economics has played an increasingly important role in all regulatory policies. It seems nothing short of quaint that in 1965 the Antitrust Division of the U.S. Department of Justice had no Economic Analysis Group, that in 1970 the FCC had no economic policy staff, and that in 1972 the Atomic Energy Commission could rule that a benefit-cost analysis of a nuclear power plant was unnecessary because the value of electricity was infinite and so would outweigh any cost. Of course, the best evidence about the increased importance of economics is the consulting issue: the conversion of so many economic experts to well-paid advocates reflects the importance of economic arguments in influencing policy.

As with interest groups, economists are more effective when they agree. If a group of economists associate themselves with their private political ideology, the impact of their advice will be limited to their ideological allies and will swing with political fortunes. Given the risk aversion of politicians, ideological victories are very likely to be tempered by compromise to avoid imposing targeted harm. In any event, the dominant political ideology of official Washington is highly unstable, so ideologically based reforms are likely to be temporary.

Unfortunately, that is probably a pointless observation. Political values are held strongly and deeply by everyone else, so why not by economists? It is most assuredly not corrupt to believe that some market imperfections impose smaller costs on society than any coercive attempt to correct them, because of one's personal assessment of the value of uninhibited contract and property rights. It is equally assuredly not corrupt to believe that regulation has produced more good than harm in ameliorating some market failures and that, if strengthened, regulation could be even more effective. Hence, economists are unlikely to see great virtue in keeping their values in check when lawyers, political officials, and interest-group advocates do not do so.

In addition, the market tends to reward ideology handsomely. Not only consulting but also much research philanthropy comes from sources that already know the answer and seek the least implausible economic argument to support it. Whereas that circumstance has always prevailed to some degree, it is certainly a more important phenomenon in the 1990s than it was before 1975, when the consensus emerged that structurally competitive industries should be deregulated and that economic incentives were more effective than technical standards for attacking environmental, health, and safety problems. Economists who saw no great evil in the fact of administrative regulation nevertheless agreed with the first, and economists who saw in all administrative processes a dangerous loss of liberty could nonetheless support the latter, despite knowing that a regulator would decide how many permits would be traded. In many areas of current regulatory controversy, no similar compromised common ground has been identified.

Nevertheless, a great deal of room for professional consensus still remains. Defining an enhanced role for benefit-cost analysis in environmental, health, and safety regulation is certainly one, but here the recommendation has to be policy-neutral. Mandatory benefit-cost analysis will not enjoy consensus support if it is perceived as a stalking horse for vastly reducing the scope of regulation by imposing greater process costs on agencies without giving them more resources. In addition, the procedures for formalizing mandatory benefit-cost analysis must self-consciously include provisions that address the lack of trust in economic policy analysts. Two ways to gain consensus support for mandatory benefit-cost analysis are to insist that all benefit-cost analyses make use of a common set of assumptions and undergo peer review and to require that, after a few years, major benefit-cost analyses undergo a retrospective review and update. Both functions should be assigned to an office outside the regulatory agencies.[33]

Likewise, consensus probably could be achieved on how to introduce more competition into the utility sector—in local telephone service and all elements of energy utilities. Procompetitive regulation has succeeded in the past, even if at a slower pace than some would have preferred. Examples are the relaxation of entry and pricing rules by the Civil Aeronautics Board in the late 1970s,[34] the gradual relaxation of administrative controls over cable television from 1972 until the industry was deregulated by the Cable Communications Policy Act of 1984,[35] the new national trading system for sulfur oxides and the local trading system for sulfur and nitrous oxides in Los Angeles that were made possible by the Clean Air Act Amendments of 1990, and, in a few states, the introduction of an independent electricity generation industry that grew out of the highly regulated and inefficient system for allowing independents to undertake cogeneration and to build facilities using renewable resources.[36]

Both the use of benefit-cost analysis and procompetitive regulation are making headway, although progress is slow. Most likely, progress will continue, and economists will help it along. Maybe the rate of progress would increase if the ratio of objective research to didactic policy advocacy were a little higher.

Notes

1. The exact dating of the reform period is, of course, arbitrary. A reasonable date for the beginning of the reform period is the Civil Aeronautics Board's Domestic Passenger Fare Investigation in the early 1970s and a reasonable ending date is the formal death of the Civil Aeronautics Board in 1984.

2. See Joskow and Noll (1994).

3. See Hahn (1989).

4. See Viscusi (1994).

5. See Foster and Hahn (1995).

6. See Portney (1990).

7. See Burke (1997).

8. See Hahn (1996).

9. See Joskow (1991, 1998) and Utility Data Institute (1995).

10. See Ferejohn and Shipan (1989).

11. For a more complete survey, see Noll (1989).

12. For a more complete development of these ideas, see Noll (1989).

13. See Bernstein (1955) and Lowi (1969).

14. See Downs (1957) and Olson (1965).

15. See Stigler (1971), Peltzman (1976), and Becker (1983).

16. For a more complete statement and test of that hypothesis, see Peltzman (1989).

17. See Eads (1972).

18. See Peltzman (1989).

19. For a more thorough analysis of the Telecommunications Act of 1996, see Joskow and Noll (1999).

20. For another perspective on emissions trading in Los Angeles, see Foster and Hahn (1995).

21. See Crandall and Winston (1994).

22. See McCubbins, Noll, and Weingast (1989).

23. See Levine (1981).

24. See Downs (1957).

25. The discussion in this section of the acquisition of politically relevant information by voters is developed more completely in Noll (1993).

26. See McCubbins and Schwartz (1984).

27. See McCubbins, Noll, and Weingast (1987, 1989) and Lupia and McCubbins (1994).

28. See Noll and Weingast (1991).

29. See, for example, MacAvoy (1970) and Noll (1971).

30. See, for example, Riker (1987).

31. See Johnson (1989–1990).

32. Their willingness to undertake a reform that drove several airlines to bankruptcy may be an exception, but more likely that outcome was not foreseen; certainly the economic studies of the 1970s did not predict that outcome.

33. For example, Breyer's proposed superregulatory agency could perform those functions (Breyer 1993). See also Hahn and Litan (1997).

34. See Levine (1981).

35. See Crandall and Furchtgott-Roth (1996).

36. See Joskow (1989) and Cameron (1995).

References

Becker, Gary. 1983. "A Theory of Competition among Pressure Groups for Political Influence." *Quarterly Journal of Economics* 98: 371–400.

Bernstein, Marver H. 1955. *Regulating Business by Independent Commission.* Princeton: Princeton University Press.

Breyer, Stephen G. 1993. *Breaking the Vicious Circle: Toward Effective Risk Regulation.* Cambridge: Harvard University Press.

Burke, Thomas. 1997. "On the Rights Track: Americans with Disabilities Act." In *Comparative Disadvantage? Domestic Social Regulations and the Global Economy*, edited by Pietro S. Nivola. Washington, D.C.: Brookings Institution Press.

Cameron, Lisa. 1995. "Limiting Buyer Discretion: Effects on the Price and Performance of Long-Term Contracts." Graduate School of Industrial Administration, Carnegie Mellon University, photocopy.

Crandall, Robert W., and Harold Furchtgott-Roth. 1996. *Cable TV: Regulation or Competition?* Washington, D.C.: Brookings Institution Press.

Crandall, Robert W., and Clifford Winston. 1994. "Explaining Regulatory Policy." *Brookings Papers on Economic Activity: Microeconomics*: 1–31.

Downs, Anthony. 1957. *An Economic Theory of Democracy.* New York: Harper.

Eads, George C. 1972. *The Local Service Airline Experiment.* Washington, D.C.: Brookings Institution.

Ferejohn, John A., and Charles Shipan. 1989. "Congress and Telecommunications Policy Making." In *New Direc-*

tions in Telecommunications Policy, edited by Paula R. Newberg. Durham, N.C.: Duke University Press.

Foster, Vivien, and Robert W. Hahn. 1995. "Designing More Efficient Markets: Lessons from Los Angeles Smog Control." *Journal of Law and Economics* 38: 19–48.

Hahn, Robert W. 1989. "Economic Prescriptions for Environmental Problems: How the Patient Followed the Doctor's Orders." *Journal of Economic Perspectives* 3(2): 95–114.

————. 1996. "Regulatory Reform: What Do the Government's Numbers Tell Us?" In *Risks, Costs, and Lives Saved*, edited by Robert W. Hahn. New York and Washington, D.C.: Oxford University Press and AEI Press.

Hahn, Robert W., and Robert E. Litan. 1997. *Improving Regulatory Accountability*. Washington, D.C.: AEI Press and Brookings Institution Press.

Johnson, Leland L. 1989–1990. "Dealing with Monopoly in International Telephone Service." *Information Economics and Policy* 4: 225–47.

Joskow, Paul L. 1989. "Regulatory Failure, Regulatory Reform, and Structural Change in the Electric Power Industry." *Brookings Papers on Economic Activity: Microeconomics*: 125–208.

————. 1991. "The Evolution of the Independent Power Sector and Competitive Procurement of New Generating Capacity." *Research in Law and Economics* 13: 63–100.

————. 1998. "Electricity Sectors in Transition." *Energy Journal* 19 (2): 25–52.

Joskow, Paul L., and Roger G. Noll. 1994. "Economic Regulation." In *American Economic Policy in the 1980s*, edited by Martin Feldstein. Chicago: University of Chicago Press.

————. 1999. "The Bell Doctrine: Applications in Telecommunications, Electricity, and Other Network Industries." *Stanford Law Review* 51: 1249–1315.

Levine, Michael E. 1981. "Revisionism Revisited? Airline Deregulation and the Public Interest." *Law and Contemporary Problems* 44: 179–95.

Lowi, Theodore J. 1969. *The End of Liberalism: Ideology, Policy, and the Crisis of Public Authority*. New York: Norton.

Lupia, Arthur, and Mathew D. McCubbins. 1994. "Designing Bureaucratic Accountability." *Law and Contemporary Problems* 57: 91–126.

MacAvoy, Paul W. 1970. *The Crisis of the Regulatory Commissions.* New York: Norton.

McCubbins, Mathew D., and Thomas Schwartz. 1984. "Congressional Oversight Overlooked: Police Patrols versus Fire Alarms." *American Journal of Political Science* 28: 165–79.

McCubbins, Mathew D., Roger G. Noll, and Barry R. Weingast. 1987. "Administrative Procedures as Instruments of Political Control." *Journal of Law, Economics, and Organization* 3: 243–77.

———. 1989. "Structure and Process, Politics and Policy: Administrative Arrangements and the Political Control of Agencies." *Virginia Law Review* 75: 431–82.

Noll, Roger G. 1971. *Reforming Regulation: An Evaluation of the Ash Council Proposals.* Washington, D.C.: Brookings Institution.

———. 1989. "Economic Perspectives on the Politics of Regulation." In *Handbook of Industrial Organization,* edited by Richard Schmalensee and Robert Willig. New York: North-Holland.

———. 1993. "Downsian Thresholds and the Theory of Political Advertising." In *Information, Participation, and Choice,* edited by Bernard Grofman. Ann Arbor: University of Michigan Press.

Noll, Roger G., and Barry R. Weingast. 1991. "Rational Actor Theory, Social Norms, and Policy Implementation: Application to Administrative Processes and Bureaucratic Culture." In *The Economic Approach to Politics,* edited by Kristen Renwick Monroe. New York: HarperCollins.

Olson, Mancur. 1965. *The Logic of Collective Action.* Cambridge: Harvard University Press.

Peltzman, Sam. 1976. "Toward a More General Theory of Regulation." *Journal of Law and Economics* 19: 211–40.

———. 1989. "The Economic Theory of Regulation after a Decade of Deregulation." *Brookings Papers on Economic Activity: Microeconomics:* 1–41.

Portney, Paul W. 1990. "Economics and the Clean Air Act." *Journal of Economic Perspectives* 4(4): 173–81.

Riker, William H. 1987. *The Development of American Federalism.* Boston: Kluwer Academic Publishers.

Stigler, George J. 1971. "The Theory of Economic Regulation." *Bell Journal of Economics and Management Science* 2: 3–21.

Utility Data Institute. 1995. *State Directory of New Electric Power Plants.* Washington, D.C.: UDI/McGraw Hill.

Viscusi, W. Kip. 1994. "Health and Safety Regulation." In *American Economic Policy in the 1980s,* edited by Martin Feldstein. Chicago: University of Chicago Press.

About the Author

ROGER G. NOLL is the Morris M. Doyle Professor of Public Policy in the Department of Economics at Stanford University. At Stanford, he is also the director of the Public Policy Program, the director of the Program in Regulatory Policy in the Stanford Institute for Economic Policy Research, and a professor by courtesy in the Graduate School of Business and the Department of Political Science. Mr. Noll's research interests include government regulation of business and public policies regarding research and development. Currently, he is evaluating the role of federalism in regulatory policy and is conducting international comparative studies of the performance of regulatory institutions and infrastructural industries.

JOINT CENTER

AEI-BROOKINGS JOINT CENTER FOR REGULATORY STUDIES